This journal belongs to:

_____

Today we went to: _____

Date: _____ Location: _____

Today is: Monday Tuesday Wednesday
Thursday Friday Saturday Sunday

Weather

Temperature: _____

Draw the best thing about today:

_____
_____
_____

List something that you

heard: _____

smelled: _____

ate: _____

What did you see or do? _____

_____
_____
_____
_____
_____
_____
_____
_____
_____

Today's Overall Rating

☆ ☆ ☆ ☆ ☆

Today we went to: _____

Date: _____ Location: _____

Today is: Monday Tuesday Wednesday
Thursday Friday Saturday Sunday

Weather

Temperature: _____

☀ ⛅ ☁ 🌧

_____
_____
_____

Draw the best thing about today:

List something that you

heard: _____

smelled: _____

ate: _____

What did you see or do? _____

_____
_____
_____
_____
_____
_____
_____
_____

Today's Overall Rating
☆ ☆ ☆ ☆ ☆

Today we went to: _____

Date: _____   Location: _____

Today is: Monday Tuesday Wednesday
Thursday Friday Saturday Sunday

Weather

Temperature: _____

☀ ⛅ ☁ 🌧

_____
_____
_____

Draw the best thing about today:

List something that you

heard: _____

smelled: _____

ate: _____

What did you see or do? _____

_____

_____

_____

_____

_____

_____

_____

_____

_____

Today's Overall Rating

☆ ☆ ☆ ☆ ☆

Today we went to: _____

Date: _____ Location: _____

Today is: Monday Tuesday Wednesday
Thursday Friday Saturday Sunday

Weather

Temperature: _____

_____
_____
_____

Draw the best thing about today:

List something that you

heard: _____

smelled: _____

ate: _____

What did you see or do? _____

_____
_____
_____
_____
_____
_____
_____
_____
_____
_____

Today's Overall Rating
☆ ☆ ☆ ☆ ☆

Today we went to: _____

Date: _____ Location: _____

Today is: Monday Tuesday Wednesday
Thursday Friday Saturday Sunday

Weather

Temperature: _____

☀ ⛅ ☁ 🌧

_____
_____
_____

Draw the best thing about today:

List something that you

heard: _____

smelled: _____

ate: _____

What did you see or do? _____

_____
_____
_____
_____
_____
_____
_____
_____
_____

Today's Overall Rating
☆ ☆ ☆ ☆ ☆

Today we went to: _____

Date: _____ Location: _____

Today is: Monday Tuesday Wednesday
Thursday Friday Saturday Sunday

Weather

Temperature: _____

_____
_____
_____

Draw the best thing about today:

List something that you

heard: _____

smelled: _____

ate: _____

What did you see or do? _____

_____
_____
_____
_____
_____
_____
_____
_____
_____

Today's Overall Rating
☆ ☆ ☆ ☆ ☆

Today we went to: _____

Date: _____   Location: _____

Today is: Monday Tuesday Wednesday
Thursday Friday Saturday Sunday

Weather

Temperature: _____

☀ ⛅ ☁ 🌧

_____
_____
_____

Draw the best thing about today:

List something that you

heard: _____

smelled: _____

ate: _____

What did you see or do? _____

_____
_____
_____
_____
_____
_____
_____
_____
_____

Today's Overall Rating
☆ ☆ ☆ ☆ ☆

Today we went to: _____

Date: _____ Location: _____

Today is: Monday Tuesday Wednesday
Thursday Friday Saturday Sunday

Weather

Temperature: _____

☀ ⛅ ☁ 🌧

_____
_____
_____

Draw the best thing about today:

List something that you

heard: _____

smelled: _____

ate: _____

What did you see or do? _____

_____
_____
_____
_____
_____
_____
_____
_____
_____
_____

Today's Overall Rating
☆ ☆ ☆ ☆ ☆

Today we went to: _____

Date: _____ Location: _____

Today is: Monday Tuesday Wednesday
Thursday Friday Saturday Sunday

Weather

Temperature: _____

_____
_____
_____

Draw the best thing about today:

List something that you

heard: _____

smelled: _____

ate: _____

What did you see or do? _____

_____
_____
_____
_____
_____
_____
_____
_____
_____

Today's Overall Rating
☆ ☆ ☆ ☆ ☆

Today we went to: _____

Date: _____ Location: _____

Today is: Monday Tuesday Wednesday
Thursday Friday Saturday Sunday

Weather

Temperature: _____

Draw the best thing about today:

_____
_____
_____

List something that you

heard: _____

smelled: _____

ate: _____

What did you see or do? _____

_____
_____
_____
_____
_____
_____
_____
_____
_____
_____

Today's Overall Rating

☆ ☆ ☆ ☆ ☆

Today we went to: _____

Date: _____ Location: _____

Today is: Monday Tuesday Wednesday
Thursday Friday Saturday Sunday

Weather
Temperature: _____

_____
_____
_____

Draw the best thing about today:

List something that you

heard: _____

smelled: _____

ate: _____

What did you see or do? _____

_____

_____

_____

_____

_____

_____

_____

_____

_____

_____

Today's Overall Rating
☆ ☆ ☆ ☆ ☆

Today we went to: _____

Date: _____ Location: _____

Today is: Monday Tuesday Wednesday
Thursday Friday Saturday Sunday

Weather

Temperature: _____

_____
_____
_____

Draw the best thing about today:

List something that you

heard: _____

smelled: _____

ate: _____

What did you see or do? _____

_____
_____
_____
_____
_____
_____
_____
_____
_____

Today's Overall Rating
☆ ☆ ☆ ☆ ☆

Today we went to: _____

Date: _____ Location: _____

Today is: Monday Tuesday Wednesday
Thursday Friday Saturday Sunday

Weather

Temperature: _____

_____
_____
_____

Draw the best thing about today:

List something that you

heard: _____

smelled: _____

ate: _____

What did you see or do? _____

_____
_____
_____
_____
_____
_____
_____
_____
_____

Today's Overall Rating
☆ ☆ ☆ ☆ ☆

Today we went to: _____

Date: _____ Location: _____

Today is: Monday Tuesday Wednesday
Thursday Friday Saturday Sunday

Weather

Temperature: _____

_____
_____
_____

Draw the best thing about today:

List something that you

heard: _____

smelled: _____

ate: _____

What did you see or do? _____

_____
_____
_____
_____
_____
_____
_____
_____
_____
_____

Today's Overall Rating
☆ ☆ ☆ ☆ ☆

Today we went to: _____

Date: _____   Location: _____

Today is: Monday Tuesday Wednesday
Thursday Friday Saturday Sunday

Weather

Temperature: _____

_____
_____
_____

Draw the best thing about today:

List something that you

heard: _____

smelled: _____

ate: _____

What did you see or do? _____

_____

_____

_____

_____

_____

_____

_____

_____

Today's Overall Rating
☆ ☆ ☆ ☆ ☆

Today we went to: _____

Date: _____ Location: _____

Today is: Monday Tuesday Wednesday
Thursday Friday Saturday Sunday

Weather

Temperature: _____

_____
_____
_____

Draw the best thing about today:

List something that you

heard: _____

smelled: _____

ate: _____

What did you see or do? _____

_____
_____
_____
_____
_____
_____
_____
_____
_____
_____

Today's Overall Rating
☆ ☆ ☆ ☆ ☆

Today we went to: _____

Date: _____ Location: _____

Today is: Monday Tuesday Wednesday
Thursday Friday Saturday Sunday

Weather

Temperature: _____

_____
_____
_____

Draw the best thing about today:

List something that you

heard: _____

smelled: _____

ate: _____

What did you see or do? _____

_____

_____

_____

_____

_____

_____

_____

_____

_____

Today's Overall Rating
☆ ☆ ☆ ☆ ☆

Today we went to: _____

Date: _____ Location: _____

Today is: Monday Tuesday Wednesday
Thursday Friday Saturday Sunday

Weather

Temperature: _____

_____
_____
_____

Draw the best thing about today:

List something that you

heard: _____

smelled: _____

ate: _____

What did you see or do? _____

_____
_____
_____
_____
_____
_____
_____
_____
_____

Today's Overall Rating
☆ ☆ ☆ ☆ ☆

Today we went to: _____

Date: _____ Location: _____

Today is: Monday Tuesday Wednesday
Thursday Friday Saturday Sunday

Weather

Temperature: _____

_____
_____
_____

Draw the best thing about today:

List something that you

heard: _____

smelled: _____

ate: _____

What did you see or do? _____

_____

_____

_____

_____

_____

_____

_____

_____

_____

Today's Overall Rating

☆ ☆ ☆ ☆ ☆

Today we went to: _____

Date: _____   Location: _____

Today is: Monday Tuesday Wednesday
Thursday Friday Saturday Sunday

Weather

Temperature: _____

_____

_____

_____

Draw the best thing about today:

List something that you

heard: _____

smelled: _____

ate: _____

What did you see or do? _____

_____

_____

_____

_____

_____

_____

_____

_____

Today's Overall Rating
☆ ☆ ☆ ☆ ☆

Today we went to: _____

Date: _____ Location: _____

Today is: Monday Tuesday Wednesday
Thursday Friday Saturday Sunday

Weather

Temperature: _____

☀ ⛅ ☁ 🌧

_____
_____
_____

Draw the best thing about today:

List something that you

heard: _____

smelled: _____

ate: _____

What did you see or do? _____

_____

_____

_____

_____

_____

_____

_____

_____

Today's Overall Rating

☆ ☆ ☆ ☆ ☆

Today we went to: _____

Date: _____ Location: _____

Today is: Monday Tuesday Wednesday
Thursday Friday Saturday Sunday

Weather

Temperature: _____

☀ ⛅ ☁ 🌧

_____
_____
_____

Draw the best thing about today:

List something that you

heard: _____

smelled: _____

ate: _____

What did you see or do? _____

_____

_____

_____

_____

_____

_____

_____

_____

Today's Overall Rating

☆ ☆ ☆ ☆ ☆

Today we went to: _____

Date: _____ Location: _____

Today is: Monday Tuesday Wednesday
Thursday Friday Saturday Sunday

Weather

Temperature: _____

_____
_____
_____

Draw the best thing about today:

List something that you

heard: _____

smelled: _____

ate: _____

What did you see or do? _____

_____
_____
_____
_____
_____
_____
_____
_____
_____
_____

Today's Overall Rating
☆ ☆ ☆ ☆ ☆

Today we went to: _____

Date: _____ Location: _____

Today is: Monday Tuesday Wednesday
Thursday Friday Saturday Sunday

Weather

Temperature: _____

_____
_____
_____

Draw the best thing about today:

List something that you

heard: _____

smelled: _____

ate: _____

What did you see or do? _____

_____
_____
_____
_____
_____
_____
_____
_____
_____

Today's Overall Rating
☆ ☆ ☆ ☆ ☆

Today we went to: _____

Date: _____ Location: _____

Today is: Monday Tuesday Wednesday
Thursday Friday Saturday Sunday

Weather

Temperature: _____

_____
_____
_____

Draw the best thing about today:

List something that you

heard: _____

smelled: _____

ate: _____

What did you see or do? _____

_____
_____
_____
_____
_____
_____
_____
_____
_____
_____

Today's Overall Rating
☆ ☆ ☆ ☆ ☆

Today we went to: _____

Date: _____ Location: _____

Today is: Monday Tuesday Wednesday
Thursday Friday Saturday Sunday

Weather

Temperature: _____

_____
_____
_____

Draw the best thing about today:

List something that you

heard: _____

smelled: _____

ate: _____

What did you see or do? _____

_____
_____
_____
_____
_____
_____
_____
_____

Today's Overall Rating
☆ ☆ ☆ ☆ ☆

Today we went to: _____

Date: _____ Location: _____

Today is: Monday Tuesday Wednesday
Thursday Friday Saturday Sunday

Weather

Temperature: _____

_____
_____
_____

Draw the best thing about today:

List something that you

heard: _____

smelled: _____

ate: _____

What did you see or do? _____

_____
_____
_____
_____
_____
_____
_____
_____
_____
_____

Today's Overall Rating
☆ ☆ ☆ ☆ ☆

Today we went to: _____

Date: _____ Location: _____

Today is: Monday Tuesday Wednesday
Thursday Friday Saturday Sunday

Weather

Temperature: _____

_____
_____
_____

Draw the best thing about today:

List something that you

heard: _____

smelled: _____

ate: _____

What did you see or do? _____

_____

_____

_____

_____

_____

_____

_____

_____

_____

Today's Overall Rating
☆ ☆ ☆ ☆ ☆

Today we went to: _____

Date: _____ Location: _____

Today is: Monday Tuesday Wednesday
Thursday Friday Saturday Sunday

Weather

Temperature: _____

☀ 🌤 ☁ 🌧

_____
_____
_____

Draw the best thing about today:

List something that you

heard: _____

smelled: _____

ate: _____

What did you see or do? _____

_____
_____
_____
_____
_____
_____
_____
_____
_____

Today's Overall Rating
☆ ☆ ☆ ☆ ☆

Today we went to: _____

Date: _____ Location: _____

Today is: Monday Tuesday Wednesday
Thursday Friday Saturday Sunday

Weather

Temperature: _____

Draw the best thing about today:

_____
_____
_____

List something that you

heard: _____

smelled: _____

ate: _____

What did you see or do? _____

_____
_____
_____
_____
_____
_____
_____
_____
_____

Today's Overall Rating
☆ ☆ ☆ ☆ ☆

Today we went to: _____

Date: _____ Location: _____

Today is: Monday Tuesday Wednesday
Thursday Friday Saturday Sunday

Weather

Temperature: _____

Draw the best thing about today:

List something that you

heard: _____

smelled: _____

ate: _____

What did you see or do? _____

_____

_____

_____

_____

_____

_____

_____

_____

Today's Overall Rating

Today we went to: _____

Date: _____ Location: _____

Today is: Monday Tuesday Wednesday
Thursday Friday Saturday Sunday

Weather

Temperature: _____

_____
_____
_____

Draw the best thing about today:

List something that you

heard: _____

smelled: _____

ate: _____

What did you see or do? _____

_____

_____

_____

_____

_____

_____

_____

_____

_____

Today's Overall Rating
☆ ☆ ☆ ☆ ☆

Today we went to: _____

Date: _____ Location: _____

Today is: Monday Tuesday Wednesday
Thursday Friday Saturday Sunday

Weather

Temperature: _____

_____
_____
_____

Draw the best thing about today:

List something that you

heard: _____

smelled: _____

ate: _____

What did you see or do? _____

_____
_____
_____
_____
_____
_____
_____
_____
_____

Today's Overall Rating
☆ ☆ ☆ ☆ ☆

Today we went to: _____

Date: _____   Location: _____

Today is: Monday Tuesday Wednesday
Thursday Friday Saturday Sunday

Weather

Temperature: _____

☼ ⛅ ☁ 🌧

_____
_____
_____

Draw the best thing about today:

List something that you

heard: _____

smelled: _____

ate: _____

What did you see or do? _____

_____
_____
_____
_____
_____
_____
_____
_____

Today's Overall Rating

☆ ☆ ☆ ☆ ☆

38764130R00053

Made in the USA
Middletown, DE
11 March 2019